THE
MODERN DAY
ENTREPRENEUR

MAKING IT IN
TODAY'S WORLD OF
ENTREPRENEURSHIP

Nuance Publishing

ISBN-13: 978-0692984673
ISBN-10: 0692984674

Printed in the United States of America

THE
MODERN DAY
ENTREPRENEUR

MAKING IT IN
TODAY'S WORLD OF
ENTREPRENEURSHIP

Nuance Publishing

Table of Contents

Foreword .... *vii*

Acknowledgements .... *xi*

Chapter 1
Breaking the 'Stick to One Thing' Rule
By Angie Renee'.. 1

Chapter 2
The Shift Economy
By Cekeita Murdaugh.. 15

Chapter 3
From Horrible Bosses to the Boss of Me
By Ebony Giavonne Pollard.. 39

Chapter 4
Building a Legacy of Change
By Dr. Jiajoyce Conway.. 57

Chapter 5
Not Just a Hairstylist
By Tiffany Moneak.. 83

Foreword

This book is so right on time! I have to be honest, being an entrepreneur is so vital more than ever today. Jobs are not secure and technology is absolutely taking over. I find that when you make a decision to work for yourself, there are so many challenges that you will face. However, the biggest challenge is to not be in control of your own financial future. When you read these stories in this book, I encourage you to do your best to put yourself in the shoes of these visionaries. Have you ever been in a position where you were forced into entrepreneurship or forced to take on a new role? Maybe right now you're working a job that is not fulfilling your needs. You might be on a job where you know that you're worth more than what you are being paid. You may be in a position where you're looking for a job and you really don't want to go work for someone else. Today, you will find that there are so many ways out here to make money. People are finding solutions to so many problems which are allowing them to become financially free. If you want to be a successful entrepreneur, the key is to find a problem and solve it.

This book is definitely going to be a great start for you in coming up with ideas.

I find that the best ideas I've ever created always started with being around the right people. That's what you're going to be able to get from reading this book. When I was offered the opportunity to write this foreword, I was completely honored. I've been blessed to be an entrepreneur now for over eighteen years.

However, please know that I was very unsuccessful for ten of them. For me, I've always wanted to be my own business owner, I just really never knew what I was doing and I wasn't around the right people. I laugh at the fact that I seriously have tried more businesses than one could imagine. In fact, I gave myself the title of 'trypreneur' because I have tried it all! Things didn't change for me until I started surrounding myself with winners in the world that I wanted to win in!

Being an entrepreneur can also be very scary! You may not know when you will get paid. There may be long days. There may be times where you have to stay focused and work and work and work. When you take that leap of faith and step into the world of being an entrepreneur, know that it will be faced with challenges, distractions, and roadblocks.

However, if you would have asked me if I would change anything, I would tell you "no". This journey to success has been absolutely amazing and the fact that you have this book means that you are ready to take that step forward. Enjoy these stories and let them be a bit of inspiration for you to also become The Modern Day Entrepreneur!

Taurea Vision Avant

Acknowledgements

Supporters

Karen Carter
Houston, TX

Michele Lain
St. Louis, MO

Angela Layne
Seattle, WA

Vanda Davis
Phoenix, AZ

Kacie Starr Long
Pastor and Radio Show Host
Inspired Overflow
St. Louis, MO

Latosha Carter
St. Louis, MO

Other Modern Day Entrepreneurs

Alicia Sellman

Simply Designed LLC
Instagram: @simply_designed_llc

Ryland Gore MD MPH

rylan.gore@northside.com
www.northatlantabreast.com

Kimberly Raimi

www.scereneorganics.com

Janine Lee

President & CEO

Southeastern Council of Foundations
janine@secf.org

Jackie Heard

Surgical Technician, Business Mentor
www.employed2empowered.com

Adrianne Martin

Co-Owner

Free Flow Fitness
St. Louis, MO

Kawana Waddell
Stylist
Style-Taneous Styles
St. Louis, MO

Quincy Peoples
Barber and Hair Replacement Specialist

Instagram: @Q_ThaBarber
F.E.S Credit Repair and Tradelines
We Move People (ATL Moving Company)
Instagram: @WeMovePeople

Shequana Hughes
Shiq Assist Virtual Assisting

"Flawlessly takes on your administrative tasks so that you can focus on the things that matter most. Our services include: Executive Administrative Support, Social Media, Email, Travel, Calendar Management, Blog and Newsletter Writing, and a host of other services. Contact us for a free discovery call!"

www.shiqassist.net

Tori Nunley
Action Community Development

"Empowering the community by educating and building one family at a time; by focusing on financial budgeting planning, credit restoration, economic growth and housing resources."

Facebook: Action Development Community
www.actiondevelopmentcommunity.com

Pamela F. Harris

Connections Family Resource

"Advocacy Family Violence Resource Center that utilizes education and intervention"

Facebook: Connections Family Resource Center
www.connectionsfrc.org

Dr. Deborah "Dr. DJ" Johnson-Blake
The Writing Pad, LLC

"The Writing Pad, LLC is a writing, editing and consulting firm with a mission of offering the highest level of service focusing on proofreading, editing, and customized writing services. Some of our projects include editing dissertations, papers, letters, and developing PowerPoint and Prezi presentations. Basically, we edit anything with content. We make writing simple."

Facebook: djohnsonblake
Instagram: @drdjblake
Twitter: @djohnsonblake
LinkedIn: deborahjohnsonblake
www.deborahjohnsonblake.org

Ronisha Shead

Bizzell Development Solutions / Moms That Hustle

"At Bizzell Development Solutions, we help busy entrepreneurs create content that attracts their ideal client. Moms That Hustle was created to help moms find their passion and profit from it by starting a side hustle or online business."

Facebook: Moms That Hustle
Instagram: @MomsThatHustle
www.bizzelldevelopmentsolutions.com
www.momsthathustle.com

Kathy Hood

Marvelous Light Empowerment Association, Inc. / Woman University

"Woman University (WU) is a 'life changing' coaching program for women who are transitioning into the woman they want to, and are destined, to become. The Woman University team will Empower, Encourage, and Equip YOU to prosper! To facilitate this process, we are implementing our ground-breaking 3-Step Program – Discover, Design, and Dare! Attendance and active participation is crucial for you to receive a positive 100% return on your investment. Once enrolled, you should prepare yourself to honor your commitment. The Discover, Design, and Dare Program was designed by WU Founder, Kathy Hood. With years of experience from coaching women of all ages and ethnic backgrounds, Kathy continually came across a common thread that prevented women from living their purpose."

Facebook: Woman University
www.simplymarvelous.org
www.womanuniversity.net

Dorothy S. Travis
Next Level CEO

"The motto of Next Level CEO is 'Always Leveling Up' and we are dedicated to empowering women to successfully navigate through the various phases of transition one level at a time."

Facebook: Dorothy S Travis
Instagram: @DorothySTravis
www.nextlevelceo.org

Maleeka T. Hollaway
The Official Maleeka Group, LLC

"A Brand Communictions Firm"

Twitter: @The_OMG_LLC
Instagram: @The_OMG_LLC
www.theomg.biz

7th & Minter

"Apparel and Accessories for the Urban Soul"

Twitter: @7thAndMinter

Instagram: 7thAndMinter

www.7thndMinter.com

Tye Jones

Author, Motivational Speaker, Confidence Coach

"I am the relatable reference for the inner city and the window for the unknown."

Instagram: @_TyeJones

Facebook: Tye Jones

www.tyejoness.com

1

Breaking the 'Stick to One Thing' Rule

How it All Started

I first became an author back in 2014. I always knew I wanted to write a book, but I also thought my book would be a novel, opposed to a self-help book for women. The natural born writer in me allowed me to take my pen to another level. I first thought it would be out of my element, considering I was used to storytelling. But I quickly learned how it just flowed and the words started showing up. When I wrote my first book, *Angieology: In My Words*, I had no clue where it would take me. I was just having fun, being myself, and talking about real life issues that most women go through. I did a few book signings, but that was all I planned on doing. Little did I know, God had other plans for me. I started getting booked for speaking engagements and asked to be a guest on radio shows. I was also asked to be a columnist for a newspaper! Everything was happening so fast.

Not to mention, many people were asking me, "How do you go about self-publishing your book?" They then started asking me to help them. Just like that, a light bulb turned on. That is where my company, Nuance Publishing, was birthed. I was still working a job at the time, so I didn't take it very seriously at first. You know, I was comfortable at my job and knowing I had a check coming in every two weeks. That was my first mistake. I never gave it my all, because I had a job to attend every day. I wasn't marketing my business, nor was I telling people that I even had one! Silly, I know. Especially considering I didn't even like my job and wanted to get out of it ASAP! It's funny how we ask God for certain things that we already have right in front of our face.

My business was the start of the financial freedom I was asking for. My business was the very thing that came natural to me, without any stress or headache. It was up to me to make it happen, take it serious, and take it to the next level. I then started promoting it more and gained my first client. Let me tell you something: when you are in business and just getting started, gaining that first client/customer gives you a certain kind of confidence that you just can't explain. Once I got that client, I ended up getting another one quickly after. Now, keep in mind I was still working that job I hated. Once I gained my second client, it brought me my third client immediately, because it was a referral.

By this time, I was not only ecstatic, but excited. It gave me the wherewithal to put fire up under my butt and really take it there professionally. I then started doing research and writing down how many books I would need to publish in order to sustain my income. I felt like as long as I was making at least what I was making from my job, I'd be good. I then joined a mastermind group. Listen, when you are wanting to do different things, you have to be around those with the same mindset as you. We met once a week for six months.

During that time, I gained more knowledge and got suggestions on how to move forward. I gave myself a goal to quit my job by 2017. I achieved that goal and was able to quit in October 2016. I didn't tell a soul. The reason being, is this: you let people know what you're going to do and they aren't on the same business-minded level as you, they can quickly talk you out of it. Remember, I was already stuck on that employee mentality and receiving a guaranteed check every two weeks, so the last thing I needed was someone to reaffirm my fear. I honestly don't even remember when I finally told everyone. I think they just kind of figured it out by watching my social media. Once I put myself out there as an author and publisher, things began to change quickly. I will say this, when I took my business seriously, so did everyone else. Because of my expertise, I was able to charge more. I also incorporated writing consulting into my business. That then created a beast within itself! Adding the consulting portion to my business allowed me to service those who wanted to write a book, but needed help either getting started, or expressing themselves. This also allowed me to charge by the hour for these services. The consulting offered those a chance who wanted to work with me a more affordable option. It still was a win-win, because once I gained their trust and built a solid rapport, they would come back to publish their book with me.

Many of my clients would refer me as well. This is why having a great attitude and personality is important when working with people one-on-one. You can't blame bad service on your "employees", because you are the brand! You now have to take full responsibility for everything, be it right or wrong. Clients can't call corporate to complain, they are going to call you. Being mindful of these things are vital to your business when you are working directly with people.

When the Speaker Meets the Author, While Being the Publisher

Once I became an author, I immediately started having small women empowerment gatherings. I honestly was doing it because it was fun for me and I enjoyed enlightening women on topics and doing it in a candid way. I felt I had found my niche. As I became more comfortable in doing this and realizing I wanted to do it for a living, the universe started making things happen. I began being offered to speak at different conferences and showcases. At the time, I was still working the job that I knew I wanted out of. I continued my journey as an author and speaker. When people asked what I did, my answer was "I'm an author and a speaker." I never edified my job. It wasn't that I was ungrateful for it, because I was. I mean, that was my primary way of paying my bills. I answered that way, because I knew eventually if I kept putting it out in the atmosphere that I was that, it would come to fruition that I would *be* that on a full-time basis.

Words are indeed powerful, so I continued to walk as if I was a full-time entrepreneur. That is also around the time that I started promoting my publishing company more. If you want different results, you have to do things differently. That is exactly what I was doing… things differently. I know what you're thinking. "How can you possibly do all of those things without being all over the place? Just choose one!" Well, the answer to that is "Easy", and my rebuttal is, "Why should I?" Who says that I can't do all of those things and not make money off of them? Who is to say that I can't pursue all of my gifts and help people at the same time? I am the only one in control of what I can or cannot handle. The same goes for you and your business! Gone are the days where many of our grandparents had only one business and wouldn't dare consider pursuing another one. Though brick and mortar businesses are still around, many entrepreneurs are making a substantial amount of money right from the comfort of their own home...or smartphone...or car! Doing so not only reduces having an overhead, but in many cases, it minimizes the need for staff. Even those of us who have businesses that may need assistance from time to time, we outsource the work (I'll talk about this later).

As I stated earlier, being all of those things actually creates a beautiful, entrepreneurial marriage. They all fall in line with each other. For instance, I can be on stage and speak about being an author as well as a publisher, and not be all over the place. Being an author makes it easy for me to be a publisher, just as being a publisher makes it easy for me to speak on my company and how it works. Make no mistake about it, being a modern day entrepreneur has its ups and downs that many won't speak on, but I still wouldn't trade it for a 9-5. Both have their pros/cons and not everyone is built for it. It's totally all up to the individual to do what works best for them.

In a 'Daze' Work

I used the word 'daze' as a play on words to describe what my typical day is like. During the week, I get up at around 7 a.m. to get my daughter ready for school and drop her off. After that, I either come back home to do work, or I go to a place of business. It may be the library, a local coffee shop, or a hotel lobby. If you're wondering why I don't just go home, it's because I can be easily distracted in my comfort zone. Knowing what your distractions are is important when it comes to running your business! Being that I literally do everything from my laptop and phone, I have the convenience to work anywhere that has WiFi. Where I choose to work on that particular day honestly just depends on how I'm feeling. Once I'm comfortably on my laptop, I check emails and send out emails. Being that I do workshops, webinars, and conference calls often, I send invites out through an email blast. Once that is complete, I send out my social media posts and check messages on there. I like to make posts typically around 9 a.m., because this is usually when people are at work, but still on social media seeing what's going on. I then start whatever is on my daily planner. I could have a session scheduled with a client or it could be a day set aside for me to go over book edits for a client. Being a publisher and writing consultant, I like to make sure my clients' book content has flow and is understandable to the reader.

Depending on how much of a zone I'm in, this can go on for a few hours if I'm really into it. After I complete that task, I may go back to my social media to check comments and messages, as well as my emails again. I always check these things every few hours because I constantly put myself out there as to what I do. Therefore, I'm usually tagged by other people and have messages inquiring about my services. THAT is what you want! I like to call it a pipeline. Referrals, inbox message inquiries, and comments showing interest in my business are the first people I contact once I'm logged back in. The key is getting back to those people as soon as possible while their interest is piqued. Getting back to potential clients quickly is always a boost in your customer service skills. They will automatically believe you will handle their project in the same manner (which I do). Building that rapport before you even speak with them verbally can easily increase the chances of gaining a client.

By this time, it's almost time for me to pick my daughter up from school. If it isn't, I may go ahead and run a few errands or prepare dinner. Keep in mind, I still have not worked a full eight hour day. Because I make my own schedule by planning everything out in advance, I know exactly how much time I will have to accomplish my tasks without rushing. The key is strategically planning everything out by writing it down.

Outsourcing

Outsourcing is one of the main elements that many modern day entrepreneurs use. It's far more convenient to hire a virtual assistant to make follow up calls and emails for your scheduled appointments, than to do it yourself. It frees up your time. Now, this is not to be confused with the emails that I initially send out. This is strictly for my scheduling and follow up emails. The whole point of being a modern day entrepreneur is to have as much free time as possible, while making triple the income. The term "Work smarter, not harder" isn't just cliché. It's real and should be a motto to follow. That doesn't mean never work hard, it simply means to not work hard-*er*. Even as a small business owner, you can still run it like a large corporation and operate as CEO. As long as you are overseeing everything and making sure it runs smoothly, why not get someone who does it better for you? It only makes sense. What many entrepreneurs fail at is trying to do everything themselves. They end up working twelve hour days sometimes on their business, because they either don't trust anyone to hire, or they can't afford to pay someone for their assistance. Listen, if you are going to be slaving over your business, without the free time to even enjoy the fruits of your labor, you are seriously cheating yourself. The point is to be financially *free*, not financially bound! Hire a freelancer or assistant to help you run your business like a true boss!

If it's Easy, it isn't Entrepreneurship

If it was easy, everyone would be doing it. Honestly, that is one of the main reasons many won't jump out and create their own income, because they know it isn't easy. Though I absolutely love what I do, I'll be the first to tell you, it truly isn't all roses all the time. There are many business owners who will brag and boast about being their own boss and not having to answer to anyone, or even gloat about how much they make monthly, but they wouldn't dare tell you about the bad days. There may be times where you may not know where your next payment is coming from. Or a day when a client is supposed to make a payment, but doesn't. And if you are in retail, your expected forecast may be much lower than you predicted. But guess what? These are things that are out of your control. I say that because many will let that discourage them from starting their own business. There are risks in everything. However, with no risk, there is no reward. As I stated earlier in the chapter, though it isn't easy and has its ups and downs, I still wouldn't trade it for a 9-5. I would rather be frustrated within my own business, than upset and miserable at someone else's establishment that I am making rich, and not even being paid what I am worth.

As a matter of fact, it's those hard times and struggle moments that keep you wanting to become more successful and appreciate it more. It's during those times that I reflect on why I even made the decision to be in control of my own destiny. It makes me suck it up and put on my big girl panties. There is no one I can complain to, only a quick reality check and a glimpse in the mirror gets me pumped back up.

Though tough times may come, I still strongly encourage entrepreneurship of some kind to everyone. You always want to have something to call your own, and to have, in case something happens. And with today's economy, you can never be too safe. Create an additional stream of income by becoming a modern day entrepreneur. I guarantee that it will change your life!

Angie is an Author, Speaker, Writing Consultant, and Publisher. She also has a passion for mentoring and educating women in a very candid way. She likes to call it 'empowering with an edge'. In order to help others achieve their writing goals, she decided to start her own publishing company, Nuance Publishing, where she not only publishes books, but does writing consulting as well. In January 2017, she became a Vision Educator where she educates small business owners and entrepreneurs on How to Write a Book in 30 Days. This program allows entrepreneurs to leverage their business, as well as build multiple streams of income. Angie contributes most of her success to just simply being herself. Her witty, girl-next-door approach is what draws people to her.

🌐 www.AngieRenee.com
www.NuancePublishing.com

💬 Facebook.com/Angieology
Instagram.com/SetApartAng
Instagram.com/NuancePublishing
Twitter.com/SetApartAng

✉ Angie@AngieRenee.com
Info@NuancePublishing.com

2

The Shift Economy

Personal Preparation

"Every morning you have two choices: continue to sleep with your dreams, or wake up and chase them"
—Lisa Nichols

Let me ask you a few opening questions:

- Do you want to spend more quality time with your family and friends?
- Do you want to be paid more for the value that you bring to your work?
- Do you see yourself calling the shots, instead of having the shots called to you?
- Do you see yourself providing a service to others, while being paid well for it?

- Do you want to determine your income, instead of it being assigned to you?
- Do you have the passion, purpose, and potential, to lead your life effectively?
- Do you want to become all that you feel you already are?
- If you had an opportunity to change your life, would you?

If you answered yes to most or all of these questions, then it's time that you hire yourself. It's time for you to begin the process of transitioning. Nine times out of ten, when you work for someone else, their primary mission and goal is not to make you financially free and independent. They want to get your skills, knowledge, ability, creativity, and ideas for as little as possible — simply because your salary is directly affecting their bottom-line profits.

So, what you have to do is make the decision that you will hire yourself. The life spent in doing what you love is a different life indeed from putting yourself out for hire to the highest bidder. There is nothing wrong with working just for money for a time, but sooner or later, your soul will likely want more from you. When we depend upon someone else's structure for direction and support, we never know when it is going to shrink, collapse, or simply replace the part that we play in it. Freedom can't be demanded from others...it must be created for ourselves.

If you don't wake up with a plan, everything that's not part of your plan is going to try to work against you. The wealthiest people in the world are all entrepreneurs and according to Forbes magazine, they acquire their income from nine different industries. Who are entrepreneurs? Entrepreneurs are people who hire themselves to provide a product or service of value to this world. They don't make wages; they make profits in exchange for those products and services. Entrepreneurs are people who take chances on themselves and their ideas, inventions, concepts, music, talent, abilities, gifts, and so forth. Entrepreneurship is a mindset rooted in the desire for independence. This is the age of the entrepreneur, the dreamer, the visionary, and the people of passion. All of the ages that came before, merely set the stage for you to stand up and show off the dreams and passions within you. Think about it, with the introduction of each age, there has been a drastic change in the way we work. It is important that we understand the age in which we are now working, so that we can best adapt to it, maximize it, and eventually take a leadership role within it. The employee is a rather new phenomenon.

During the agrarian age, most people were entrepreneurs. Most children who were raised in entrepreneurial families followed in their parent's footsteps, also becoming entrepreneurs. It was during the Industrial Age that the demand for employees grew. The rise of the giant corporation is rapidly slipping into the history books as we return to our entrepreneurial roots. In today's and tomorrow's economy, one of the best things you can do to ensure that you are part of the powerful current of new wealth creation, is to become an individual entrepreneur or independent contractor. Now with the information age and creative age here, we have the benefit of all the ages that came before. Napoleon Hill, the author of Think and Grow Rich, says, "Ideas are the beginning points of all fortunes." Your idea is your "start-up" capital. If you have an idea, you can turn it into money. So, it's time you make a decision to hire you! I did.

Start Where You're At

Everyone needs a place to begin, but everyone's path starts at a different place. At the age of nineteen in 2006, I decided to become a professional bartender because I did not want my life's dreams to be dictated by the size of my paycheck. Becoming a bartender was a life changing experience. It was the bridge from my current situation, to my ideal one. I went from working five days a week making $300.00 paychecks, to working five days a week earning over $1000.00 from tips alone. Bartending was the start of my entrepreneurial journey. Working behind the bar had so many built in benefits like flexible hours along with getting to meet and know celebrities, lawyers, doctors, professionals, and other people from the community that frequented the bar. People in bar settings are much more relaxed and, therefore, more candid. On an average night, you can serve and interact with over 100 people. It became my social platform and my circle of influence started to expand. I began being offered opportunities outside of the bar. I generated an additional stream of income as a freelance bartender. The greatest benefit was the freedom! I charged what I wanted, I picked the events that most interested me, and I worked when I wanted to. Although bartending was my dream job, it was still not my dream. Many people choose bartending for private reasons. The most common are that they are studying or pursuing another line of work, in which they are not yet established such as acting, writing, or setting up their own business.

When I wasn't bartending, I submerged my mind in books on topics such as leadership, entrepreneurship, business, and personal development. I've always had big dreams. Two of my biggest dreams at the time were: 1) to become an entrepreneur by starting a business and 2) to become an author by writing a book, but I didn't know where to start. Then one day, one of my favorite quotes replayed in my head, "Start where you're at and use what you can today." At that moment, everything finally clicked. Almost every day at work, a waitress or customer would ask me to train them to bartend. I kept referring them to the bartending school that I attended. The two biggest complaints were it was too expensive and it was not compatible with their schedule. Honestly, bartending schools leave much to be desired. Through their marketing, they fool people into believing they must attend a bartending school in order to become a bartender, which is not true. That's when I decided to go to work on updating an outdated system.

I began documenting my routinized work and carefully analyzed every detail surrounding the position. In 2015, I packaged my experience and knowledge into a bartending workbook/program titled Bartender Bootcamp. Bartender Bootcamp provides on-the-job training for those lacking experience and the knowledge to be successful in the industry. My goal was to create the ultimate and most innovative hands-on training experience for aspiring bartenders and aspiring entrepreneurs. When you first walk into the training room, one student described her experience as, "Walking into a bartender's dream world!" There are stations all over with everything that a professional bartender would need to make a drink. I can accommodate thirty-six students per class. If I offer two sessions in one day, I can accommodate seventy-two students. Most bartending schools can accommodate twelve students bi-weekly. The first part of the workshop focuses on hands-on training. Students learn bar basics, how to craft the classics, and the most often ordered drinks by guests at on premise establishments. The second part of the workshop focuses on career advancement and opportunities outside of the bar. Students are taught branding, marketing, and how to generate additional streams of income by starting their own mobile bartending business. We end with a cocktail style networking reception which allows students to ask questions, share ideas, and mingle with other participants and speakers. I host the Bartender Bootcamp live training event once a month. Instead of having a brick and mortar business, I facilitate workshops which allows me to keep my overhead low and pass the savings along to my students. Working from home requires discipline and focus.

In most businesses, the level of success you can achieve is directly related to the time and effort you're willing and able to contribute. A shared industry-wide motto for event planners is, "You're only as good as your last event." When I'm not hosting an event, I'm innovating the business, networking on social media sites, and marketing from my home office using the internet. Our economy is in the middle of its greatest growth spurt in history. The internet represents one of the greatest economic revolutions in history and it's just getting started. Because of social media and the internet, big companies no longer have a big advantage. Social media has become a phenomenon beyond words. On June 27, 2017, Facebook CEO Mark Zuckerberg announced that Facebook hit 2 billion users. Now is your time to take full advantage of this low-cost (often no-cost), global and local opportunity. Business social media is the new cold call. You'll make sales, you'll create loyal customers, and you will profit from your ability to expose yourself, your thoughts, your experiences, your interactions, your value to your market around the corner, and your market around the world.

Make Money While You Sleep

Becoming an author has absolutely changed my life! I created a Professional Bartending Workbook and leveraged it to create six additional streams of income.

- I host monthly hands-on training workshops.
- I contract and provide consulting services to established bars and restaurants.
- I created an online course.
- I teach the business of bartending and sell my book in bulk to professional bartenders who want to facilitate my program.
- I coach aspiring authors.
- I coach entrepreneurs and educate aspiring youth entrepreneurs on expanding their natural talents and passions into their work while earning a living.

Coaching gives me tremendous freedom and

flexibility. It is also a very rewarding process. I consider it my life's work, because it is the vehicle that allows my spirit to shine forth. I am an advocate for financial literacy and entrepreneurship. A lot of us weren't educated on money; that's why a lot of us don't have the success we want. What did you learn about money in school? Have you ever wondered why our school systems do not teach us much, if anything, about money? Is the lack of financial education in our schools simply an oversight by our educational leaders? Or is it part of a larger conspiracy? If a person has a solid financial education, they will not cling so tightly to job security and a steady paycheck. How would your life be different right now, if you received an education on money and how to accumulate wealth?

In today's world, financial education is absolutely essential for survival. It bothers me that schools don't teach you how to build a system, but they teach you how to work for it. It also bothers me that children today are not receiving an education that is preparing them for the future they face. I believe every child should be taught entrepreneurship early on, because money and entrepreneurship are life skills. There are people who make things happen, there are people who watch things happen; and there are people who say, "What happened?" 74 percent of self-made millionaires in America, made their fortunes by starting their own companies. They created an opportunity that opened them up to wealth and so can you!

In 2017, I founded The Murdaugh Business Initiative. Students are trained on basic wealth building, entrepreneurship, and financial literacy. Head over to Facebook and join The Murdaugh Business Initiative group to connect with other like-minded aspiring and new entrepreneurs and to stay updated on upcoming events, free trainings, startup tips, and ongoing support that will help you launch, run, and grow the business of your dreams. Bartending classes are offered as one of our programs, because bartending is recession proof. When you learn to bartend, you learn a system that teaches you to think like an entrepreneur, because your income does not come from your employer; it is generated by you. The more outgoing, creative, and service oriented you are with bartending, the more money you make in tips. There is no glass ceiling on the amount of money you can make. The earning potential is unlimited.

I made the leap from entrepreneur to infopreneur by creating an information product platform. The term 'infopreneur' is a relatively new industry buzz word. An infopreneur is a person who creates, packages, and sells informational products. Informational products are offered in many formats:

• Books
• E-Books

- Special Reports
- MP3 files
- Audio Products
- Videos/DVDs/CD's
- Teleseminars and Webinars
- In-person Seminars/Workshops
- Workbooks,
- Consulting
- Life/Business Coaching
- Online Courses
- Membership Programs
- Certification Programs
- Mastermind Groups
- Speeches
- Mobile/App
- Virtually any format in which you can deliver information.

Authors who have generated wealth from selling books, have realized the need to make the transition from author to infopreneur. They have created multiple information products and developed multiple streams of income to survive in the marketplace. Revenue is often considered the primary benefit to information products. E-learning is a 107 billion-dollar industry. While money is a big motivator, there are numerous advantages you may not have considered. Passive income, which is another term for residual income, is income that continues to flow after the work that created it has been completed. In other words, residue remaining from the original effort. Rental property income is the most traditional example of passive income. Once an information product is created and the distribution is automated, sales can occur with little additional effort, and potentially, for the rest of your life. This could free us from the necessity of trading hours for dollars and allow us to build long-term financial security for our families and ourselves. Any money you invest into building a residual income is the wisest investment of all. Publishing a book also enhances your credibility and can lead to speaking engagements and media interviews. Many authors treat their books like fancy business cards, using them to open doors of opportunity.

Do it Today

Is your work getting you to where you want to go in life? Are you doing something you love? As long as you're taking inventory, this is a good time to sit down and list your passions, strengths and experiences. What kind of work gives you the most joy? What have you loved doing most in the past? What skill can you offer to other people? How can you take what you love most and turn it into an entrepreneurial business? Robert Kiyosaki is probably one of the most intelligent business minds that I know. I have been a student of his Rich

Dad principles for many years now. I can remember when I read his New York best seller Rich Dad, Poor Dad for the first time. He mentioned in his book how people who get up each morning and go to a job to make money to pay bills alone are in a financial rat race, because they will never catch up. In the book, he states that the word job really stands for "just over broke." Robert captured and harmonized the way that most people really feel about their jobs. People work jobs to try to make ends meet, but because of over spending and variable expenses, those ends keep moving farther apart. Most people end up having more month at the end of their money, instead of more money at the end of the month! It's a revolving cycle that is increasingly difficult to get out of. That's why so many financial gurus call it the rat race.

There are millions who earn just enough to survive, but cannot afford to live. Many people with jobs cannot afford their own home, adequate health care, education, or even set aside enough money for retirement. There was a study conducted in USA Today on employers and employees in the workplace. The study confirmed that most employers paid employees just enough money so that they would not quit. The study also confirmed that most employees worked just hard enough for employers that they would not get fired. In between all of the "just enough" behavior, everybody ends up settling. In the job world, you are mainly doing a task. That's why jobs, and sometimes even careers, are often so easily replaced with technology, since keeping you employed and making you financially prosperous is not the goal of most corporations. They will quickly replace you if technology advances enough to replace tasks that you do manually.

In the past, people looked to jobs for security and for a consistent paycheck. But now, with corporate downsizing, mergers, and offshoring, even job security has become a joke in the real world. Don't let other people's ventures or businesses sidetrack you from what you really want. Don't wait for others to validate and affirm you. I decided that my dream was worth the sacrifice of my time and that I would do whatever was necessary to manifest my dreams. Never underestimate who you are, what you know, and what you are capable of. The technology gap is where you will find the greatest potential for growth. As an entrepreneur, this is where you will find the greatest opportunity. This is where the great majority of the next millionaires will come from in the years ahead of us. Make sure you are always working in a business where you can use and leverage your skills for the highest return. The world is changing so fast and if you don't take steps to grow, you will be left behind. We're living in a new economy, so we can't operate with old habits. In the new information society, where the only constant is change, we can no longer expect to get an education and be done with it. There is no one education nor no one skill that lasts a lifetime now. Like it or not, the information society has turned us all into lifelong learners. Our attitudes toward change and learning are critical to our effectiveness.

It is important to ask yourself:

1. Are you being paid by the month, the hour, the minute, or the second?
2. Are you earning money eight hours a day or 24/7?
3. If you stop working, will money continue to come in?
4. Do you have multiple sources of income?
5. If you are an employee, are you working for an employer who is being left behind financially?

Only you can honestly answer those questions. Only you know if you are financially satisfied with your own life. Only you can daily make changes in your life. Transitioning from your job to your dream is probably one of the biggest decisions and action steps you will ever make. It's important for you to know that while choices are critical for success, once you decide, you need to act! Once you decide to transition in the mind, you must then go there in the body! And this is where the real magic happens. See, most people do decide! They say, "Yes, I want to be an entrepreneur. I want to own my own business and start taking a leadership role in my future!" However, what typically happens is that their actions don't line up with that new choice. So they continue to manifest sameness, instead of manifesting change and difference. Make a conscious decision about how you want to live your financial life.

Self-Directed Study

There is a difference between making money and generating wealth. Do you want to just generate money or do you want to be wealthy? Wealth is a person's ability to survive so many days forward. If you stop working today, how many days could you survive? Wealth is measured in time, not in dollars. Most people are one skill away from great wealth. A single skill developed could take you from the bottom of your income bracket to the top. The only skill most people know, is to work hard.

How much time do you spend each day building your wealth? Wealth comes from big goals and sustained action toward those goals every day. Many people start with big goals. Yet after they run into a few problems or get distracted by other things that compete for their attention every day, they lose focus on their goals. To keep your goals alive, you must take action every single day. Your daily habits are the reason for your wealth or your poverty. Your future is created by what you do today, not tomorrow.

Here is a questionnaire to help gauge your mindset. Refer to these questions frequently and always be honest with yourself.

1. Do I have the mindset and drive to become an entrepreneur?
2. Am I contributing a sufficient amount of effort to acquire my desired results?
3. What actions am I currently executing to ensure I reach my goals?
4. What changes can I make to my lifestyle to improve my path towards success?

If you cannot lead yourself, you will not be able to lead others. Lost time can never be regained. Can you find four to ten hours a week that you could spend on your financial education? Chances are, you can. The question is: will you? What you can learn in college is specialized knowledge, but even this can often be learned more quickly and effectively through "Self-directed study." Assuming you have the initiative and discipline, self-directed study has a lot to offer. First, it puts you in control. You learn what you want to learn, when you want to learn it, because you want to learn it. It sparks creative synthesis and enhances retention because you learn with an eye toward applying what you learn. Self-directed study, especially when combined with some form of apprenticeship, is often superior to the formal lecture/exam mode of training. Where you need new skills, try to get into a program where you can actually practice what you learn. Skills are best learned through practice. Even when you are seeking specialized knowledge, stay away from relying entirely upon books. As much as possible, learn from people who are doing what you want to do. You could work as an apprentice, study on your own, take targeted classes, or you could hire a coach. Professionals have coaches, amateurs do not. You hire a coach when something is important to you and you know you need to be pushed, held accountable, and challenged to go beyond your resistance, laziness and limitations. Success leaves clues, but the right mentorship accelerates growth.

Entrepreneurship has become more accessible than ever through technology with all of the tools available today. In 2007, Time Magazine said, "The computer is the person of the year!" Because for the first time in the history of the world, everyday people have access to information that wealthy people have and that really makes a difference. You now have access to information that will allow you to build the life you want and so desire. We have an abundance of knowledge at our fingertips. This is the first time in history that an individual person can start a business themselves, run it themselves, and make a good living from home. Home-based businesses are one of the fastest growing segments in our economy, and that trend will only continue. As the age of the corporation which began barely a century ago, now gives way to the age of the entrepreneur. If you have a skill at a job right now, you can turn it to a contractor basis. All you have to do is sell yourself and your skills.

In the beginning, you don't have to quit your job to start a business. Use your current position as a place of preparation, not a place of frustration. Your job is your first source of capital to invest. With a few hundred bucks on the side, you can start your own projects after hours, write a book, or learn a new skill and see if people will pay for it. Start the process of personal development and you can make yourself more valuable to the marketplace. Learn to work harder on yourself than you do on your job. If you work hard on your job, you can earn a living. If you work hard on yourself, you can make a fortune. Promise yourself that you will practice your dream until you master it! Just as if you wanted to learn medicine, mechanics, or law, you would have to study the subject in detail for a long time in order to master it!

Follow Your Dreams

Making money should not be the sole purpose of starting a business. It's about creating something of value which you are passionate and committed to. "Begin with the end in mind." This means to begin today with the image, picture, or paradigm of the end of your life as your frame of reference or the criterion by which everything else is examined. How different our lives are when we really know what is deeply important to us, and keeping that picture in mind, we manage ourselves each day to be and to do what really matters most. Our businesses are expressions of our highest values. Your better future is a dream for you and your family. Evolving a fresh idea requires work. For some people, work is hard. Anything that is hard can cause stress and anxiety. Hard work, anxiety, fear, rejection, risk, and stress, all are part of the process of being an entrepreneur.

Aspiring entrepreneurs never succeed due to:

1. Laziness
2. Bad habits
3. Lack of education
4. Lack of experience
5. Lack of guidance
6. Bad attitude
7. Bad influence from friends and family
8. Lack of focus
9. Lack of determination
10. Lack of courage

Zig Ziglar says, "You don't have to be great to start, but you have to start to be great!" You will make some mistakes along the way, but it's impossible to learn without making mistakes. The key is to learn the lessons of those mistakes, and not let them take you out of the game. Look at failures as a learning opportunity.

Learning a system to create wealth and control my financial destiny has given me the opportunity to change lives by sharing my knowledge and experience with others. Doing work I love gives me the fuel to keep going when times get rough. When you set a clear goal for yourself that you really want, and you begin working toward it, day by day, you intensify your desire and deepen your belief. Every step forward deepens your conviction that it is possible for you. This is the meaning of the statement, "A journey of a thousand miles begins with a single step." Resources are attracted to movement. Resources don't come towards you until you start moving.

"Believe while others are doubting. Plan while others are playing. Study while others are sleeping. Decide while others are delaying. Prepare while others are procrastinating. Work while others are wishing. Save while others are wasting. Listen while others are talking. Smile while others are frowning. Commend while others are criticizing. Persist while others are quitting."
– William Arthur Ward

Cekeita Murdaugh is an educator, entrepreneur, business coach, and consultant. She is best known as the founder of the Murdaugh Business Initiative, a private financial education company that provides personal finance and business education to people through workshops, books, coaching, and online courses. Murdaugh has dedicated her professional efforts to the field of entrepreneurship. She has a sincere desire to help solve the problem of the growing poverty gap in America. She is on a mission to impact and empower over one-million men, women, and children in their work. Cekeita believes that everyone has the ability to create their own economy. The Murdaugh Business Initiative is a starting point for anyone who wants to control their financial destiny. Students are trained on basic wealth building, entrepreneurship, and financial literacy. The material is the result of Cekeita's dedicated 16+ years of studying, knowledge, and expertise.

Facebook: Cekeita Murdaugh

CekeitaMurdaugh@gmail.com

3

Horrible Bosses to the Boss of Me

When I consider all the twists and turns my life has taken in thirty-something years, it becomes more evident to me that all roads were leading me here. Free-spirited and full of ideas, I was destined to become an entrepreneur. I faced many obstacles and experienced a few false starts, but eventually, I made it to the summit and there would be no reason to look back.

From Under Mama's Roof to Under Uncle Sam's Thumb

As the child of an incarcerated man and a member of a blended family, I grew up feeling like a caged animal. I never seemed to fit in anywhere and I always felt as though I had to be less me to be received. By the time I graduated from high-school, it was as though the Tasmanian devil had been unleashed. I joined the military and hightailed it out of my hometown of Saint Louis, Missouri like I'd been set on fire. Other than holidays, weddings and funerals, I had no intentions of coming back.

Barely legal and still wet behind the ears—as the old folks say—being a member of the Armed Forces was a vast experience, to put it mildly. I obtained several skills that I still use to this day. I learned the importance of keeping a detailed paper trail (because you never know when you'll have to hand someone a few "receipts") and how to work under pressure. I grew thick skin and gained a certain level of discipline, although there would always be room for improvement in this area (remember, I was and am very free-spirited).

Even though I had some positive experiences and gained great skills that still serve me well, I also encountered racism, ageism, sexism and sexual harassment. The military is where I would also learn the definition of *rape culture*, in a very personal way, when a guy who lived several doors down from me broke into my dorm room and attempted to sexually assault me. When questioned by my superiors about the incident, they asked me, "What were you wearing when he broke in?" as though what I was wearing in the privacy of my dorm room somehow incited a break-in and attempted rape.

Shortly thereafter, I separated from the military with a general discharge and found myself right back in Saint Louis.

Horrible Bosses

Feeling like an epic failure, I returned home and took various jobs to make ends meet. I had no plan, no goals, and no direction. I was wandering around aimlessly through my early twenties and growing more frustrated with each passing year.

At the time, the easiest jobs to get were in the retail industry. So, I took a job at a large retail chain and stayed there for about three miserable years. I hated that job, but it kept money in my pockets, and until I could figure out what I really wanted to do with myself, it would have to do.

My last year there, I received a promotion to a department manager position. My new supervisor was unhappy about the promotion. She was hoping for a different person to get the job and made it painfully clear that she would have preferred the other young lady who had been considered for it. I didn't know this woman very well, so I tried not to take her behavior personally. Instead, I decided I would do my best at the new position and eventually she would realize that I was the best woman for the job.

Unfortunately, my new supervisor would never give me the chance to show her what I could do. She would undermine me at every turn, loudly berate me in front of customers and purposely undo all my hard work, then tell the store manager I wasn't doing my job. Her disdain for me became so obvious, other employees began to complain to management about the way she treated me.

It was too late, though. My supervisor's behavior had begun to remind me of some of the trauma I'd experienced in the military, and as much as I did not want to give up, I ended up stepping down from the position. I began looking for a new job and left the company a short time later.

Because I had a love for all things clerical and administrative, I worked various office jobs for several years. I was in school, working on a degree in Business Administration, when I landed a job as the executive administrative assistant for a non-profit organization.

I enjoyed working there, because I felt like I was contributing to a cause. But, being the youngest woman and only one of three black women in a predominantly white office, I was soon met with ageism and racism, once again. From comments about my hair to implications that I must have grown up in "the ghetto" in a single-parent household, to being questioned on if I was going to vote for, then Senator Barack Obama, simply because he was black, it became difficult to end my work day without having been insulted at least twice.

Still, the ultimate insult came when the executive director decided to add more tasks to my workload, causing me to work extra hours and cut into my evening school schedule.

"I can only miss one day of school out the month or I'll be kicked out of the program," I told my supervisor.

"Well, Ebony," she said, "I understand wanting to get your degree and all, but work has to be your priority right now."

I was infuriated. Here this woman was telling me to put my education on the back burner while she had been fully able to pursue her education.

The next day, I spoke with the executive director and told her the same thing I had told my supervisor. "Ebony," she said, "it's my way or the highway on this." They were forcing me to choose.

I chose the highway. I credit this experience for striking the match that would eventually light the fire that fuels my passion for entrepreneurship today.

The Epiphany

About a year and a half later, I obtained a position as the regional administrative director for a real estate investment firm. The CEO of the firm was struggling to maintain order. A mutual business contact suggested that the CEO hire a strong administrative professional to handle the daily operations of the company and boost the waning confidence of its clientele. Once the CEO was on board with bringing someone on, our mutual business contact recommended me for the position.

A few weeks later, I was hired, and let me tell you, I truly thought I had arrived! I was being paid an ample salary. I had a nice office and an important title to show for my talent and extensive experience in the administrative field. I even obtained my real estate license to be more of an asset to the company.

I was told that the position came with the promise of a corporate apartment and opportunities to travel around the country to establish new offices and maintain order at the existing out-of-state offices in Tennessee, North Carolina, and Texas. By that time, I was the single mom of a one-year old and I was living at home with my parents and younger siblings.

I had no car of my own and was driving my sister's car to work every day. With the generous salary I was being paid, I would be able to purchase a car and maintain a home of my own again.

It felt like this was it. It seemed like I was in a stable place and I could finally exhale like the late Whitney Houston's character, Savannah, in the movie "Waiting to Exhale," as she danced her New Year's Eve away with a beautiful stranger. But, also like Whitney's character, my sigh of relief was cut short by the proverbial sucker punch to the gut.

I wasn't made privy to the deeper inner-workings of the company, but after many phone calls from disgruntled clients—some threatening to sue—it became clear that something wasn't right. Unbeknownst to me, the company was a corrupt house of cards on the verge of collapse.

The more I questioned the CEO, the more cryptic and evasive the answers became until my boss began to outright avoid me. In fact, it was not uncommon for me to come to work and discover that I was the only one at the office on any given day.

One day, after not seeing my boss for weeks, I realized that I was going to have to resign from my position. The clients were out for blood and they didn't care who they had to take down to get it. If the company was corrupted, there was no way I was going to go down with it! The day I decided to resign, I went to my office, closed the door then sat at my desk and cried from the beginning of my shift until it was time to go home. I was tired and crushed.

I didn't want to spruce up my resume again. I didn't want to re-enter the job-hunting world, looking for the golden career from which I could retire. I didn't want another boss. I wanted to be my *own* boss. However, that came with risks I wasn't sure I was ready to take. But, I had to make a quick decision because the house of cards was beginning to topple with me inside.

A fire began to burn on the inside of me. I was tired of thanklessly working to further someone else's vision while ignoring my own. I realized that I had never been content with the "9 to 5" lifestyle and perhaps horrible bosses were God's way of showing me that He'd forged a different path for me, a path I hadn't considered before. It was time to take a leap of faith.

The Write Agent LLC

I resigned from my position as the Regional Administrative Director, and with the guidance of a business mentor, I began to establish myself as a full-time licensed realtor in the state of Missouri. I wasn't fully aware of it at the time, but this was the beginning of my journey as an entrepreneur.

My family was skeptical about my decision. I was told numerous times that I needed to "get a job." In fact, during a heated discussion, one relative told me that I needed to, "grow up, get a *real* job, and a place of my own." I was deeply hurt, but I continued to move forward with my decision and began to think of other ways to make money.

Two years after taking that leap of faith, I founded a company called The Write Agent LLC. At the time, The Write Agent was to be a hub for all my business endeavors. In January 2017, I narrowed the company's focus and The Write Agent LLC became a real estate transaction coordination and virtual assistance firm.

The Write Agent LLC was designed for real estate agents who love to sell homes, but don't love the paperwork involved. The company works with local agents who need what's called a "transaction coordinator" to handle all the administrative details associated with the listing or purchasing of a home.

Things were off to a great start until I sustained another proverbial blow to the gut.

When Life and Business Collide

I didn't feel anything. There was no fear. There was no panic. There was only an overwhelming calm as I accepted the fact that the little red car that was careening toward me, at highway speed, was not going to stop. I didn't alert my then four-year old, who was happily singing to herself in the backseat, that we were about to be in a car accident. I just waited. Then it happened.

I watched in my rearview mirror as the little red car sped toward us. It hit us and I immediately looked back at my daughter who threw her hands up and shouted, "OH," in surprise. The impact of the red car jerked us sideways and into the SUV that had been cruising in the next lane.

It was over in the blink of an eye.

Shaken but concerned for my child, I hopped out of the car and ran to the rear passenger side door to get her out. It wouldn't open. Now I was panicking. There was a gasoline can—the true cause of the accident—lodged up under my car. It had fallen off a truck and I was unable to avoid hitting it. I didn't know if there was fuel in it. All I knew is that it was stuck under my car, we had just been in an accident, and I couldn't get my baby out of what I was afraid could be a ticking time bomb.

Witnesses ran to my aid, pulling my daughter out of a window and taking her out of harm's way. The driver of the SUV that my car was pushed into, lovingly stroked my back as the shock of what had just happened kicked in.

There was so much chaos. The highway was now like a parking lot. So many people asking so many questions. All I could think was, "Lord, what am I going to do now?"

I had *just* re-launched The Write Agent LLC, with its new focus, the month before. I had also just moved out of the home I'd shared with my ex to a new home. Many of my belongings, including my work laptop and business cellphone, were inside the car and had been destroyed by the impact. The trunk of my car was completely smashed in and much of the clothing, shoes, and small household appliances that had been inside it were strewn across the highway.

My car was clearly totaled. Even with the insurance to pay off the remainder of my car loan, I wasn't going to be able to replace my car right away. This meant that some of the mobile services offered by The Write Agent would have to be suspended.

I was still in shock as they loaded my daughter and me into an ambulance. "That was scary," my daughter said, "But, we're going to be okay. God protected us, Mommy."

"Yes, He did." I managed to reply. Yes, God had protected us. We walked away from a very bad accident. But, how was I supposed to run a business with my car and several key items needed for that business now destroyed?

This was a pivotal moment for me and The Write Agent LLC. I could "take my ball and go home" or I could suck it up and get through it.

Staying the Course

It would be five months before I would be able to replace my car. During that time, I conducted meetings through conference calls or video chats. I found ways to still provide some of my suspended services. I managed to get around many of the obstacles that I was presented with following the car accident.

However, there were still some skeptics who tried to "encourage" me to let The Write Agent go and get a "real" job. I was even offered a job that would have been a terrific opportunity for someone else. But, I had chosen to have faith in myself and in the life of my business. If I abandoned The Write Agent for the assurance of a bi-weekly paycheck, I was going to be stuck building someone else's empire for the rest of my life. No, thank you!

"People must think I'm crazy to stick this out." I said to myself one day.

I *was* crazy! I was crazy enough to believe that I could do it. I was crazy enough to believe that I could build a legacy to leave to my daughter. I was crazy enough to believe that I could set a strong example for her to follow and *exceed*. I wasn't going to be able to do that by giving up!

"I can't be the only female entrepreneur that's hit an extremely rough patch and needs some encouragement," I said to a friend, "I want to find a way to encourage others to keep going even when things get hard."

Rising from the Wreckage

That night after talking to my friend, I dreamt about the car accident. There was wreckage everywhere. None of the cars on the highway were moving. I could hear people screaming and the sirens of emergency vehicles wailing as my poor little white sedan sat crushed in the middle of it all.

Out of nowhere, a woman rose from the wreckage. She wore a beautiful wedding gown trimmed with glistening jewels. Her back was to me, but I knew she was me because the dress had been one I picked out for a wedding that never happened (another story for another time). The bride that rose from the wreckage began to glide through the pieces of twisted metal like they weren't even there. Her arms were outstretched and I could feel a sense of strength emanating from her. She continued to glide towards the cars that were waiting for the debris to be cleared so that they could continue their journey to their destinations. Her arms remained outstretched. Then I woke up.

I'm a dreamer. Those closest to me know that when I dream about a thing, it usually means something. I instinctively knew that this dream was a message to rise from my wreckage and encourage others to do the same.

The Birth of the Mad Mompreneur

The concept of The Mad—as in crazy—Mompreneur was birthed from this dream, and in late 2017, I will unveil her, for all the world to see, with a website and blog launch and other announcements for what's to come in 2018.

Social media tends to make the lives of female entrepreneurs look glamourous. We don't always see what it took for our favorite entrepreneur to get to the place she's in now.

The Mad Mompreneur exists to be real about the ups and downs of entrepreneurship and inspire women entrepreneurs to stay the course when the going gets tough! So, stay tuned!

The Boss of Me

As for The Write Agent LLC, the company is still going strong and making moves that will position it for growth in 2018. I could have taken the obstacles that presented themselves as roadblocks, keeping me from making it to my desired destination. But, instead, I chose to see them as stepping stones to something greater. Those obstacles taught me to push past discomfort and continue to reach for better.

I love what I do. Being an entrepreneur enables me to be there for the things that matter most, those "you had to be there" moments. It puts me in a better position to give my daughter my undivided attention when she comes home from school instead of being too depleted to love on her after giving my all to someone else's dream. Entrepreneurship brings a balance to my life that I didn't have when I worked a 9 to 5. I am the boss of me!

Now, I will be the first person to say that entrepreneurship isn't for everyone. We all must forge our own paths and I'm never one to shame anyone for choosing the "9 to 5" lifestyle. But, for those of you within whom the fire of entrepreneurship burns bright, I encourage you to stay the course when things get rough. Don't give up after a loss! Keep pushing toward the win! Create a plan and implement it. Don't bite off more than you can chew. Be strategic in the moves you make, and even when the going gets tough, *tough it out*!

This lifestyle comes with its own set of joys and sorrows, but they are well worth it for the balance and freedom you can achieve by being your own boss.

Take the leap. Stay the course. Be a boss. Be *your* boss!

Ebony Giavonne Pollard is a mother, writer, blogger, owner of The Write Agent LLC, creator of The Mad Mompreneur blog coming in November 2017, and The Mad Mompreneur Book Club for Women Entrepreneurs. She is passionate about encouraging women to look beyond their circumstances, negative or positive, to find their purpose. Ebony has led small groups and hosted "ladies' empowerment sessions", for broken and discouraged women, and is in the process of developing a networking group for women entrepreneurs in her local area. Her bubbly personality and humorous disposition often puts people at ease within minutes of meeting her. But, make no mistake about it, she takes a no-nonsense approach to encouraging others to be the best version of themselves!

- www.diaryofamadmompreneur.com
- Facebook.com/TheMadMompreneur
  Instagram: the_mad_mompreneur
- TheMadMompreneur@gmail.com

4

Building a Legacy of Change

Owning It: What is it That I Do?

I can recall one of my mentors saying to me at the age of nineteen that, *"What you do is not who you are, but who you are will make and shape everything that you do."* This did not make much sense to me at the time, as I was still trying to figure out me, my life, and truly what it meant to be a professional nurse.

As you know, wisdom comes with time and experience, and at this very moment in my life, I can see the manifestation of these words in my life now as I have come to a place of understanding, embracing, and absorbing my own true purpose in life. All my life for as long as I can remember, all I wanted to do was take care of and help people. I only saw my life as being that of a healthcare provider, whether it be a physician or a nurse. Helping people is natural to my core.

So who I am at the very essence of my being is a nurturer, a provider, a caregiver, a consoler, an encourager, a motivator, a source of light, and a hope to others. I love to educate, empower, and esteem others towards personal and professional transformation, of becoming their greater self and fulfilling their life's purpose. One of my main missions is to help women fall in love with themselves, and discover who God has called and created them to be. Entrepreneurship, for me, is about the reach back and the give back.

Manifested Purpose

What I have come to realize, is that I was not in search of my purpose. *My purpose* was waiting for me to show up and be a present and willing participant. All those attributes I saw within myself, and as the one thing I was supposed to be, has not changed for me; I have evolved and grown personally and professionally, and have come to learn the importance of mastering my life. I am still all of those things and so much more, but these attributes have contributed to, *"What do I do now?"* and *"Where do I see myself continuing to go?"*

By profession, I am an advanced Nurse Practitioner, Doctor of Clinical Nursing Practice. For over seventeen years, I have taken care of people with cancer; and throughout this time, I have trained others to become advanced practitioners by serving as clinical faculty for several academic institutions, and as their professional mentors.

However, what I never saw or even knew would ever be a part of my life, is being a licensed Evangelist. This call on my life has now evolved to include: being a personal and professional certified life coach for women, speaker, author, and educator. What I have come to realize, is that the plans I have for my life have not necessarily ended, but they have begun the start of the plans that God has ordained for my life. If anyone would have told me that fifteen years ago I would be a preaching, teaching, speaking, Licensed Minister (Evangelist), and Certified Christian Life Coach, I don't know that I would have believed them. That is not what I ever envisioned or believed for my life.

Yet, here I am founder of *Changing From the Inside Out Ministries, LLC (CFIO) and The Epitome of A Woman Life Coaching Success Academy. The Epitome of A Woman Life-Coaching Success Academy* is a faith-based life-coaching program that focuses on the personal, spiritual and professional development, empowerment, and transformation of women who have made the decision to become the masters of their lives in pursuit of purpose. My coaching programs help women construct and carry out a unique plan for key areas in their lives, so that they may live a life of success and experience the happiness, joy, wholeness and completion in which they were designed to live. This is a platform that has afforded me the opportunity to serve as a speaker, educator, coach, teacher, preacher, mentor, and consultant. This step of faith in this endeavor to help impact the lives of other women, saved my life and renewed my hope in the true purpose of my life.

Interestingly enough, CFIO is the manifestation of my own journey through life's trials, challenges, tribulations, and ultimately the evidence of what I have been doing for years as a Doctor of Clinical Nursing Practice or "Dr. Jia", as I am affectionately known to many. As Dr. Jia, my degree has an emphasis on "outcomes and practice change." It is my sincere interest in seeing and experiencing the outcomes and positive changes in the lives of individuals that I have been privileged to counsel, coach, or mentor. This is a drive that keeps me wanting to empower others to reach their greater potential. I have been able to take what many would just see as a profession and their 9-5, and integrate my skill-sets and training into a productive, profitable platform that exceeds my work in private practice.

From the works of being an online faculty educator and career mentor to students all across the globe at several different academic institutions, a consultant to pharmaceutical companies developing new market products for the healthcare sector, public speaker, preacher, author, and a Certified Christian Life Coach to women from all walks of life, I have transformed from novice-to-master of my life; all while building a legacy of significance and success for my children, grandchildren, and generations to come. The works of my hands have been blessed and ordered to change and impact so many lives throughout my career and entrepreneurial endeavors. What I saw as just taking care of people, and initially on the terms of other people, has now become my baby to birth, shape, and mold my life as well as the lives of so many others, especially women. My journey to restoration, wholeness, deliverance from past disappointments, hurt, and onward to successful living, has not always been easy. I did not always have a mentor, coach, confidante, or community of women supporting me. There were some tough lessons I had to learn on my own. There were some places of pain I have had to endure on my own without another sister's wisdom or support. There have been times when I wanted to walk away from it all and never look back, because it always seemed to be a lop-sided game of favoritism and "who you know" in order to succeed.

Yet, the very things that God has delivered me from and gave me a second, third, and fourth chance at, are the same things that I have been gifted to do for another. I am a firm believer that when we are willing and ready, God turns our mess into our best to help us towards a greater space and place of self-fulfillment and goal attainment. I am a firm believer that when we show up and are willing to submit to the process, God opens up the windows of heaven before us.

Professional and Personal Christian Life Coaching

Changed From the Inside Out (CFIO) targets specifically women as it relates to personal, spiritual, and professional life coaching and mentorship, as this is the demographic that I am called to serve. I have a passion and drive to see women become who God says they are. *"Commit to the Lord whatever you do, and your plans will succeed, (Proverbs 16:3)"* is a spiritual principle embedded in the "Epitome of A Woman Success Life Coaching Academy." This is such an important foundational principle, because as an overcomer and now women's Christian Life Coach, I do not believe that there is anything in life that we do which will succeed apart from God and His provision; regardless of being personal, spiritual, or professional.

Far too often, I have seen many women just settling

for the subservient life that has been offered, because for some of us, we were only told to go to school and get a good college education. This creates a burden in my heart for women, because not only do I know what it is like to get a "good" college education, I know what it is like to hide behind a college education and feel like this is all I will ever have, do and be, even when all else fails.

Now, hear my heart, I am not knocking college preparation, as I believe in the power of education and its value. I have no regrets to my formal education, as it has prepared me to be a well-educated, and empowered woman, as well as an expert in my field(s).

However, it can become a crutch for some very talented and gifted individuals, who never see themselves beyond their degrees, yet they desire to do so much more. Then there is the other side of the story where not only did that woman not see education in the cards for her life, but she never even saw being or doing anything great with her life. These are the women that I carry in my bosom.

CFIO exists to serve and empower women to move beyond the false facades of fear, disbelief, and doubt, so that they may gain clarity and precision to encourage them along their journey towards taking their life back on their own terms. The end result is goal development, attainment, and fulfillment within themselves. This is the charge upon my life to lead my fellow sisters towards this place of greatness…God ordained greatness.

As a personal life coach, I have the wonderful opportunity to share in the journey of the lives of women who are now about the business of owning their lives, their destiny, and their purpose. These are the women that are ready to go from *novice to mastery* in their life's purpose. This is accomplished through a structured, but self-paced, online course that enables my clients to take their time based on their commitment in the program, to grow and develop from the inside out.

My coaching academy allows women the opportunity to take an introspective look at who they are from the perspective of starting with truly coming to understand who they are for real. They recognize their spiritual design and what that means to their personal success, who they are as a person, and why are they here. The coaching process allows women the opportunity to purge their past hang-ups and detriments. They develop a personal vision blueprint that brings to life the vision that God has put into their hearts. God already knows the plans that He has ordained for our lives. He, and the rest of the world, are waiting for the manifestation of our gifts, talents, and skillsets to show up.

The other aspect of what I do within my coaching programs are related to helping women that are either in a professional career, seeking one, or starting to establish one. I help execute and enforce a roadmap of getting to where they see themselves and how they plan on getting there. I commit my clients to overcoming their hindrances and detriments that may be preventing their success and obstructing their greatest potential from coming forth!

I do not see personal and professional coaching as two separate entities to the individual or services that I offer, because I am a firm believer in the power of personal development in order to prepare us for our future destiny. *Changed From the Inside Out* is a faith-based organization that takes the word of God and integrates it into tangible practices with sound principles, tools, and resources that help women to personally develop and transform themselves mentally, physically, spiritually, and financially.

CFIO helps women show up to their God-ordained purpose and to a life they don't just like, but that they love. Each coaching session is personalized depending on the goals of the client, but the key principles focus on: 1) Design. How God formed women, and 2) Development. What women believe God has called them to do, who He has called them to be, and how to get there.

As an experienced advanced practitioner for over seventeen years, I am able to offer women sound advice in making career decisions. Sometimes, as women we are waiting for the perfect time to move forward in our lives with our career aspirations and goals. Whether it is returning to school, becoming an entrepreneur, returning to work, or starting a new endeavor (i.e. book writing, mentoring, coaching etc.), many women are seeking the extra support, experience, and leadership of a coach to support them. What I offer my clients from this perspective, is my experience and resources as a professional career woman who has balanced many hats for a very long time: as academic faculty, practicing clinician, minister, entrepreneur, wife, mother, and grandmother. The key start for many of my clients is coaching them through the important process of assessing where they are in their lives "in the right now" and from the perspective of time, sacrifice, and commitment. *What can they truthfully give to the endeavor in order to be successful? What are they willing and able to sacrifice short-term for long-term benefit and success?*

CFIO is a safe place. It is a sanctuary for women to come discover their greater version of self without judgment. I don't fix people. People come to me when they are truly ready to be committed to make significant life changes for the better, embark upon new endeavors, and are seeking a higher level of accountability, guidance, and experiences beyond themselves. My vision and focus is to empower and help women show up to their greater version of self, learn to express who they truly are, and *master* being their greatest version of *woman* to the fullest.

Novice to Mastery: Getting Started as an Entrepreneur

To call myself an entrepreneur, I had to be sure that I truly understood what this term meant. There are so many self-defined definitions of 'entrepreneurship' and I have yet to find one that is the same from one person to the next.

However, one that I finally found that I fit into, and believe most "true entrepreneurs" do as well, was defined by Merriam-Webster. Webster states, *"An entrepreneur is a person who starts a business and is willing to risk loss in order to make money, or one who organizes, manages and assumes the risks of a business or enterprise."* This is a definition I can embrace, because it makes sense to me as it relates to how I got started and restarted.

First and foremost, I must say that I never saw myself as owning anything beyond my clothing, shoes, home, car, and my bank accounts. These are some of the easiest things to obtain in life from the simplest to the greatest. They don't require much effort, will, risk, or education. They are things, possessions, and what we call "stuff." I was good with this until I had a great woman of faith speak into my life and say, *"Your gifts will make room for you, and it will start with a book, and from there God will build, grow, and develop your platform."* I will tell you that before she could get to the period, I was on the floor. Why? The confirmation was soul-shattering. I knew what God had shown me about the turn and shift that my life was going to take, I just did not believe I could do it. Who would listen to lil' ol' me? My shift was coming.

November 2012, God reminded me that He did not deliver and restore unto me all that He had for me to be silent. It was at that time that I took pen to paper and I released my first book, *"Changed From the Inside Out."* This book was my release on life, as it spoke to some deep dark places and times in my life that I did not want to share, but at the same time knew I had to. The release of *"Changed From the Inside Out"* was a season of growing up and truly becoming liberated. This was the beginning and building of *"Changing From the Inside Out"* as a viable entity, brand, and presence before the world. This was my initial focus in 2013 at my book release.

The bird took off, but landed very soon, because I wasn't ready mentally. I was not ready to take the risks that were involved in building a business where I would need others. I am just being honest. I did not want the rejection, the scrutiny, the risk of losing money, time, and poorly committed people. I just did not want it!

So for about two years, *"Changing From the Inside Out"* was a name with a website and a book! It was a painful two years, because this was my baby, and the longing on the inside of me to do so much more, it was like a toothache that would not go away.

I watched as others were taking off, building and growing. Books, businesses, conferences, coaching, and mentoring was popping up everywhere around me. What was my problem? The problem that I can see now, was that I did not believe or dream big enough. I was too busy comparing myself to others and not believing in my very own vision and dreams. I had mastered how to encourage and empower everyone else, but somewhere in the mix I lost my own groove. I forgot about the present that was on the inside of me waiting to be opened.

Yet, I am so grateful on today that is not my same story. After I got up off the floor from the conference... there was work to be done.

My Industry/Field

The different aspects and facets of my days are many as my day starts with a busy clinic day of seeing patients from 8:30 a.m.- 6:00 p.m. in addition to my online academic responsibilities.

However, before I leave my home office, I am

answering emails from my clients and students, posting my daily inspiration to my social media forums, setting my forums to automatically send out posts, editing my newsletters and capture page links…all before leaving my home.

Throughout my day, I schedule appointment follow-ups with my mentees and clients as needed, with my dominant days of coaching calls being hosted on Tuesdays and Thursdays. I spend time coaching my academic students as well regarding their career goals and professional pursuits.

During the evening, starting about 8:00 p.m., I work in my online coaching academy posting links, videos, resources, and tools. I speak with my enrolled clients, re-check emails again from my academic and coaching students, my coach, and ministry. I set scheduled time to write personal and professional works both for ministry and for CFIO. These are the scheduled and predictable events of my day. It does not include unscheduled events of prayer calls, impromptu phone calls with my mentees and coaching clients, and business demands of working on the growth and productivity of my company, and my very own time being coached.

On average, my nights end at about 1:30 a.m. I purposefully schedule down-time and days to do nothing but work on personal development for me and my family. I am a firm believer that I must be the change that I preach, teach, and educate others to be. Some look at my schedule and call it insanely busy, but I call it productive. I believe that the time that we are so blessed to be graced with each day should be used to continually evolve to be our greatest selves. There is an expected purpose, promise, and destiny that is awaiting us all, but it must be perfected and crafted by working at it.

Balance is essential, and it is so important to know the limitations of what you are able to do efficiently and proficiently. Sometimes, that will mean saying no to some things, and being deliberate in scheduling "me" time, and family time. It is just as important to remember that success does not come easy, and that there will be some sacrifice of time, some sleepless nights, and even some moments when you mind the grind and have to remind yourself of your "why." Not everyone is going to co-sign our vision and dreams, but the depth of our dreams, goals, and aspirations must exceed the challenges that we will face; including the naysayers that will seek to tear down what we build and believe in.

Understanding the Joy & Happiness of Being an Entrepreneur

I don't believe there is any one word that I could

attribute to describing what it means to me to call something of this magnitude my own. What I have established as an entrepreneur for myself and in collaboration with others is often times surreal to me, because I still at times have to absorb and internalize that others believe and subscribe in my vision, talents, gifts and ministry. The magnitude of my vision for *CFIO* exceeds my own mindset at times, because I know that God has called me to impact others beyond my very own sphere of influence. I know and trust that God has called me to a great purpose to impact the lives of the masses. I can remember the first customer I had purchase one of my custom pieces of jewelry (when I use to handcraft jewelry). I was like *"Wow! You really want to purchase this from me? You trust my talents to this degree?"* Not only did they trust it, but they kept coming back with personal requests and referrals. This gave me the confidence to showcase at events, conferences, and women events on national scales with the ranks of *Ice* and *Cookie Lee* Multi-Level Marketing Companies.

Yet, the amazing thing that came from this endeavor, was that God was continuing to show me who He had truly created me to be, and what He was preparing me for in terms of impacting the lives of others on a much greater scale than I ever imagined. Jewelry-making helped me to engage, and to step out of my comfort zones of being introverted. It was greater than the jewelry itself. It was about becoming comfortable with me and who I was as a woman. It was about building my confidence, trusting in my gifts, talents, and abilities. This coming into knowing myself was a soul-high of matchless joy, peace and serenity that only came when I embraced my self-worth, true calling, and purpose.

So, here I stand today building my platform for *Changing From the Inside Out Ministries* that is now birthing, "*The Epitome of A Woman Success Life Coaching Academy.*" This is exhilarating and breathtaking to me, because I love what building this online program means to the lives of other women who will take my principles, teachings, and resources, and integrate them into their personal and professional lives for sustainable change, transformation, and goal attainment. The satisfaction that comes with building and then growing something from scratch is not anything someone can give you, be purchased, or caught on sale. It creates a feeling of completion, fulfillment, and significance. What I have committed unto the works of my hands comes from my soul. It is the one thing I would do, and have done, even when no one has paid me for it.

The joys of entrepreneurship for me rest in knowing that what God has graced me to do belongs to me. It affords me the privilege to build a legacy for my children and generations to come. It allows me to be as innovative and creative as I desire; to disseminate my information for the empowerment of the lives of women from all walks of life, and choose my platform for engagement of my message. I am living out my dreams on my terms, boldly and confidently without apology. Even when the road looks a little bumpy at times, and when things don't look like what I planned each and every time, the vision is still mine to start all over again with a fresh and new outlook on a blank canvas to keep pushing forward.

The fruit that has manifested of my labor is refreshing. It brings my heart a relentless happiness to see the seeds that I have planted in my life and the lives of others come to fruition. I am humbled at the thought that God would use the mess of my life to be a message that transforms the lives of other women.

There are days when the grind is real and I step back to wonder if it is worth it. But then, when I look at the lives that I have been so privileged to impart into, and the women that God has allowed my path to cross, connect and knit with as a result of sticking to my "yes"; that I gave my vision to educate, empower and esteem women to be who they were created to be, and live as they were destined to live, I am renewed, replenished, and restored to a place of perseverance where giving up is never an option! When the business is yours, you become the *who, what, when, where, and why* of it all. The perk in this is that I do not have to compromise myself or the vision of what I have been charged to do within my business, nor do I have to co-sign or ascribe to someone else's vision for me. I have the honor and privilege to collaborate with others who are like-minded and have no inhibitions about being different or unique, and the exception to the rule is to live out their life's God-ordained purpose. No longer do I have to believe that greatness is for another and not for me. Because what comes with entrepreneurship or ownership of your very own creation, is manifestation of the greatness that is already on the inside of you. My greatest perk for me through my business is that my daughters, grandchildren, and great-grand children will look back one day, and say that I left a legacy of change, a legacy of difference, a legacy of a going against the odds of trials and tribulations, a legacy that gave volume and a voice to principles of greatness, success, significance, power and purpose! When it's your baby, you get to raise that baby on your terms!

The Take Home

Complacency, trials, and tribulations are dream stealers…if we allow them to be. These three negative attributes can be dream snatchers if we don't acknowledge them for what they are. We must not sanction them to be visitors and take up space, our time, and our talents. They create comfortable positions and stability in someone else's legacy, all while negating our own sincere dreams and deepest places of fulfillment.

Complacency can keep us bound into funneling and growing the visions and dreams that do not matter to us and can cause us to never stop, look, or listen to what is valid, relevant, and real to our very own future.

Complacency has a time and place of relevancy, but it should not be where our life stops. We never see beyond where we are or where we are destined to be if we don't move outside of our comfort zones. Furthermore, the trials and tribulations of our lives are experiences that we should learn from to be the better version of ourselves. Thus, I suggest starting a journey towards entrepreneurship.

Entrepreneurship allows individuals to engage with who they truly are. I say this, because it is impossible to step out and build anything if you don't know who you are and what it is you are supposed to be doing, who you are called to serve, and what it is you were created to do. I never saw this for myself and could not even initially embrace my mind-set around doing something outside of the traditional workplace, but when I took the first step towards the core of my dreams, I began to live, build and grow beyond any limitations that were creating road blocks. *I got out of my own way.*

If there is anything that you cannot stop thinking about, anything that goes deeper than just an emotional decision, or a meantime hobby, but seeps to the core of who you are and gives you a natural high to engage in it, to talk about it, to think about it, to see it and just to be in the presence of it…you need to be doing it! Making this move to go from novice-to-mastery of your life cannot be about who has given you their stamp of approval or is standing in line to salute what you have decided to do…*for you*. There will always be a reason of why not to do something different? There will always be a head-butt to shifting with the shift of life, and that is even more of a reason to press ahead with your dreams and aspirations.

Yet, what I have come to appreciate about moving from novice-to-mastery and owning it, is that what's for me, is for me. I don't have to rob Paula to pay Paulette, and no one will show up for my life and embrace my greatness but me. Is that you? Can you co-sign to your own life's purpose and promise by stepping out into the realm of being that modern day entrepreneur? Never mind the disapproval of others, your life assignment is for you. It is about you and was ordained just for you. Life and our purpose are always waiting for us to experience it and not just exist in it. We are not waiting for our lives to show up to meet and greet us. We must have the tenacity, unction, boldness, confidence, and perseverance to show up to the better version of ourselves. We must go forth in our callings of entrepreneurship which ultimately leads us towards operating in our greatest gifts and our callings of purpose and promise.

So, I challenge you as you read the words on these pages, to step out towards your place of greatness and fulfillment. It is time to be the boss on your terms, through your own eyes, and with your own signature. We should never spend more time on funding and fueling the dreams of others than we do on our own. Comfort keeps us contained, but not always complete.

The move towards entrepreneurship is not easy, and it is a process of pruning, preparation, and remolding that takes our all to make it work. Yet, it is a worthy transition that leaves a legacy of purpose and not pain, innovation and not the traditional. Our fingerprints are unique. The world is waiting for yours and mine to make its imprint on the lives of others that are anticipating the manifestation of our gifts. Our tests are not about us and our gifts are not for us to keep opening, but they are for a greater thing beyond ourselves. So, why not try entrepreneurship? Why not challenge the greater on the inside of you that is waiting for you to pull back the layers of stagnancy towards the layers of static and dynamic change? Why not be the extraordinary version of you that is screaming to be unveiled? Take the step of faith that is greater than your fear. Fear and faith cannot co-exist, but faith will always lead us where fear cannot linger.

So, never mind the bad days that may surface on this journey, or even some of the weights of building from scratch that may ensue. What you put your hands to that you can call your own cannot be exchanged, undermined, belittled, or price tagged. A 9-5 can be our starting points, but they should not be the defining points of our success. What another will demand of you should not supersede what you are willing to demand of yourself to be great, because you are! It's time to Engage, Establish and Execute!

Dr. Jiajoyce Conway is a woman truly after the heart of God, who has been given the ministry of deliverance, restoration and empowerment. She is a woman of God who is motivated and dedicated to spreading the Gospel of Jesus Christ that the lost may be saved, transformed, and delivered towards a place of wholeness. She is a Licensed Evangelist of the Gospel, and Certified Christian Life Coach through the International Christian Coaching Association. She is the wife of a 22 year marriage, mother to four beautiful children, grandmother, published best-selling author, educator, womanpreneur, mentor, educator, and currently a practicing Doctor of Clinical Nursing Practice Practitioner for over 17 years.

She is the founder and CEO of Changing From the Inside Out Ministries, LLC and The Epitome of A Woman Success Life Coaching Academy, which is a Christian Life Coaching Program for women seeking faith-based personal and professional life coaching. She is also the co-founder of Greater Beginnings Female Mentoring Group with Min. Phyllis Trafton

🌐 Website: www.jiaconway.com

💬 Facebook: Jiaconway

✉ changedfromtheinside@gmail.com

CHAPTER

5

Not Just a Hairstylist

Who is Tiffany-Moneak?

For as far back as I can remember, I have always had a heart of service, leadership, and creative thinking. I think I was somewhere around twelve years old when I started my first job at my Uncle's convenience store back in my home town of Jackson, Alabama.

"I've always wanted to go the extra mile." I can remember being in the store during what is known back home as "hunting season." This is when people in my community would get up early in the morning and suit up to go hunting. Usually during the winter months.

On Saturday mornings, they would stop into the store to fill up on their favorite snacks, which in my eyes was not going be enough food to fill them up for the day, so I came up with the idea of starting a breakfast stand outside of the convenience store where I would sell coffee, hot chocolate, and a hot breakfast to the hunters. I shared the idea with my mother and she helped me to pull it all together. My mother is a force to be reckoned with when it comes to serving, so quite naturally, I inherited that trait. I began selling hot breakfast plates for $5. Then in the afternoon when the hunters would come through at lunch time, I would have a hot dog stand set up for them to purchase. Coming from such a small community with only two convenience stores in the area, I saw the need and I took action. That was just the beginning of my journey into entrepreneurship.

At the age of sixteen, I was faced with one of the hardest and most embarrassing times of my life. I became pregnant with my son (who is now seventeen and about to graduate high school! Praise God!) After struggling to finish high school, and now having my son to take care of, I had to put quite a few of my dreams on hold to do what I had to do in order to provide for me and my son.

At the time, I was very fortunate to have my parents to help with my son so that I could attend beauty school and get my cosmetology license to do hair. I made the decision to go to hair school, because this was something that came easily to me as I was already really great at "doing hair." I always knew that I wanted to own my own hair salon, but I never really thought of myself as an entrepreneur.

I graduated from Beauty School and in 2003, I moved to Atlanta to pursue my dreams to own a salon. Little did I know, God had a much greater plan for my life! I am living proof that anything is possible if you just believe and trust God. When it comes to my life, I have had to overcome so many obstacles from surviving abuse, divorce, being broke and broken, a single mother of four to losing my brother in 2015, and four months later being abandoned by my husband to being homeless and having my car repossessed. One thing that I do know for sure, is that I am an expert when it comes to surviving and starting over! God has opened so many doors of opportunity for me and I am grateful that He has blessed me with divine connections. He has put me in the right place, with the right people, at the right time.

Currently based out of Atlanta, Georgia. I provide high quality, on demand, professional beauty and haircare services and products to elite industry professionals with limited time on their hands. I can go to their home, office, or special event. I also teach service based industry professionals how to effectively market their new or existing business, how to *stand out* in their field, and turn their primary profession into "Multiple Streams of Income."

How I Got Started

I always knew that I had a natural born leader buried deep within, and I always knew that for some reason, I always *stood out*! But I really never thought of myself as an entrepreneur. Although I was very good at styling hair and I loved the money that I made doing it, I always knew that it was not just about being a great hairstylist, but that it was indeed a God given gift. As I stated earlier, I relocated to Atlanta and in 2005, my dream became a reality! I was able to open up my very first salon.

Great, right? *wrong*! The location sucked. I was so excited to open my own salon that I never once thought about location, business plan, marketing or any of those very important factors that should always be considered when starting any type of business. After months of struggling to keep up with the expense of running the salon, and having to hear my then-husband complain about how much money we were wasting trying to keep the salon afloat, I decided to close the doors and pursue a career in the medical profession. At least with that I would have consistent income, right? *wrong again*! This was so not the right move. I was absolutely miserable, because I felt like I had been put in a box. I felt as though I was fulfilling someone else's vision for my life.

So, needless to say, that quickly came to an end shortly after my externship. In 2010, after surviving domestic violence and a horrible divorce, I decided to go back into the salon to work full time as a stylist. In 2012, I opened my second salon, a smaller salon and was able to keep things running smoothly. After only being open for about a year, I found out the owner of the building/space I was leasing had sold the building and all the tenants would have to move out or pay double the rent. So, back to square one. That is when I decided enough is enough and I started my own mobile salon business. Still having no idea how to really market or who my target market would be.

Later on in my career, after spending countless hours and dollars on non- effective marketing, I decided to invest in a business coach. This was the best decision I could have ever made when it came to my business. She helped me to gain a clear sense of direction as to where I wanted to take my business. She helped me to regain my focus. In order to be a successful hairstylist, not only do you need to be able to style and care for hair, you also need be effective in marketing your service/ brand, but you must first know and identify your target market. Who is it that you will serve and what is it that they need. Since then, I have hired several coaches for different areas of my life, which has taken my career to heights that I could never have imagined.

A Day in My World

My formula for creating a successful life as an entrepreneur and single mother of four, has been simply this: God first, then family, then career. I am a firm believer that whatever you do first sets the tone for how the rest of your day will go. This is why I am very committed to setting aside the time to shut off all vehicles for distraction at certain times during my day. I'm a very spiritual person, so for me, early mornings are very sacred for me and my family. I'm usually up around five a.m. I like to get up about an hour before the house wakes up just to give myself some quiet, uninterrupted time to meditate and pray before getting the kids up and off to school. Our morning commute is usually the time that my kids and I take to verbally pray together and express things that we are grateful for. This is always interesting, because the kids are usually still half asleep and they really talk to God as if they were talking to their Mommy. It's one of the most precious moments of my day.

Once I have gotten the kids all dropped off, Part 2 of my day begins! I like to start off part 2 of my morning with a little inspiration. It could be anything from a book, my favorite song, a positive presentation/sermon or just simply listening to the Holy Spirit lead and guide me through His wisdom. I usually take one to two hours on Sundays to prioritize my weekly and daily tasks according to what I have on my calendar. That way I get to spend less time during the week on planning, and have more time to focus on family and income producing activities. Every month I set a goal of how many people I want to connect with that are going to help my business continue to grow. Then from that goal, I break it down into how many people I need to talk to each week, then how many people I need to talk to each day. Having gone from beauty industry professional to beauty industry expert, to author, speaker, and educator all within a matter of months, my career has catapulted to levels I could have never dreamed of or imagined! I am currently the CEO/Owner of a successful On-Demand Mobile Haircare Company. I'm super excited to launch my new luxury line of custom hair units, "Wigs So Fly" in Fall 2017. 2018 is sure to be the year to be connected with everything that God is doing in the world of entrepreneurship!

Loving What I Do

Although being an entrepreneur has its ups and downs, I absolutely love the flexibility and freedom I have to be me in every aspect of my life. For me, it's not just about being a great hairstylist, but it's more about the experience that is given with each service! As a hairstylist, I love the feeling of making someone feel beautiful and watching their confidence soar! As a beauty industry expert and business success coach, I enjoy helping my students take that very thing that they are passionate about and show them how to turn it into profits. I love showing others how to plan and build successful businesses with little to no start-up money!

The Benefits

One of the main perks to being an entrepreneur is that *You are your own B.O.S.S (Business Owner Serving and Succeeding).* Other great benefits include, but are not limited to: Being able to set your on schedule, being in control of your own time and money, you get to see your work and your gift transform lives, and you get to live out your God given purpose here on this earth so that you can enjoy life in the fullness of its abundance!

Personal Development

I will be the first to say that everyone is not cut out for entrepreneurship. If you are someone who is persistent, persuasive, disciplined, and you possess a good strong work ethic, then you may want to consider becoming an entrepreneur. The first step though, is to really seek spiritual counsel. If you are considering becoming and entrepreneur, be sure that you take some time to pray and ask God what it is that He created you to do.

Then, I suggest that any and every one considering entrepreneurship, to invest in a great coach/mentor! Not just any coach. Notice I said a *great* Coach. I have several coaches/mentors for different areas of my life. I found that having a coach has been one of the major keys to my success as an entrepreneur. My only regret is not having invested in coaching earlier in my career. Personal development is also a *big plus* when it comes to being an entrepreneur. Always be teachable. Be a learner forever. All great leaders must first be a great follower. If you are faithful over the small things, God will make you the ruler over many things.

Employee vs. Boss

Although being an entrepreneur has its share of struggles, I would never trade it in for a traditional 9-5, because living off one stream of income is just not safe anymore. I've seen it happen too many times. Families torn apart from the loss of a job due to the company downsizing, health issues, or some other reason beyond their control. Entrepreneurship gives you the freedom and flexibility to be constantly in what I call the "State of Flow", meaning you don't have to live in a box. You have the power and authority to create your own wins, whether big or small! You have the ability to change your business model to fit your own personal lifestyle. It's yours! You own it! You have the power to *make it work*!!

Tiffany-Moneak is an Author, Speaker, and Beauty Industry Expert/Educator with over 15 years' experience in her field. She is no stranger to the world of entrepreneurship. Her passion and consistency to seek continued education has played a major role in her success as an entrepreneur.

Graduating from Beauty School in 2003, Tiffany became a licensed master cosmetologist and later went on to train under the direction of celebrity stylist/beauty expert Sherita Cherry of "Genesis Hair Art" in Atlanta, GA.

Tiffany has undoubtedly had her share of ups and downs when it comes to life and business. As a result of her struggles and challenges, she has found a way to master her gift and creativity by seeking out her true God given purpose here on this earth! Helping to transform the lives of Men and Women all over the world by helping them to move from a life of brokenness, despair, and financial struggles into a life of abundance and wealth by searching out God's true calling on their life.

Instagram: @SalonMoneak
www.facebook.com/AuthorTiffanyMoneak
www.facebook.com/SalonMoneak

www.ingramcontent.com/pod-product-compliance
Lightning Source LLC
Chambersburg PA
CBHW032325210326

41519CB00058B/5813